The Life of a Narwhal

Katie Peters

GRL Consultant Diane Craig,
Certified Literacy Specialist

Lerner Publications ◆ Minneapolis

Lerner Publications
An imprint of Lerner Publishing Group, Inc.
241 First Avenue North
Minneapolis, MN 55401 USA

For reading levels and more information, look up this title at www.lernerbooks.com.

Main body text set in Memphis Pro 24/39
Typeface provided by Linotype.

Photo Acknowledgments
The images in this book are used with the permission of: © dottedhippo/iStockphoto, pp. 3, 4–5, 6–7, 12–13, 16 (center, right); © dottedyeti/Adobe Stock, pp. 8–9; © AndreAnita/iStockphoto, pp. 10–11; © Petr Slezak/Shutterstock Images, pp. 13 (fish), 16 (left); © wildestanimal/Adobe Stock, pp. 14–15.

Front cover: © dottedyeti/Adobe Stock

Library of Congress Cataloging-in-Publication Data

Names: Peters, Katie, author.
Title: The life of a narwhal / Katie Peters.
Description: Minneapolis : Lerner Publications, [2025] | Series: Let's look at polar animals (pull ahead readers - nonfiction) | Includes index. | Audience: Ages 4–7 | Audience: Grades K–1 | Summary: "Did you know that a narwhal is a type of whale? Vibrant photographs and engaging text bring these interesting animals to the surface. Pairs with the fiction title, Norman's Deep Dive"—Provided by publisher.
Identifiers: LCCN 2023031594 (print) | LCCN 2023031595 (ebook) | ISBN 9798765626283 (library binding) | ISBN 9798765629314 (paperback) | ISBN 9798765634769 (epub)
Subjects: LCSH: Narwhal—Juvenile literature.
Classification: LCC QL737.C433 P48 2025 (print) | LCC QL737.C433 (ebook) | DDC 599.5/43—dc23/eng/20230713

LC record available at https://lccn.loc.gov/2023031594
LC ebook record available at https://lccn.loc.gov/2023031595

Manufactured in the United States of America
1 – CG – 7/15/24

Table of Contents

The Life of a Narwhal

A narwhal is a kind of whale.

Many narwhals have a tusk.
A tusk is a long tooth.

A narwhal lives in the ocean.

It swims under the ice.

It dives down to find fish.
It eats the fish.

It swims up to breathe air.

Did You See It?

fish

ice

tusk

Index